iGlobal Geometry: Practice Workbook

iGlobal
Educational Services
Believe.Inspire.Transform.

To order, contact iGlobal Educational Services, 13785 Highway 183, Suite 125, Austin, Texas 78750
Website: www.iglobaleducation.com
Fax: 512-233-5389

©2016 by iGlobal Educational Services, Austin, Texas.

ISBN-13: 978-1-944346-12-6

Printed in the United States of America.

How to Use This Practice Workbook

iGlobal Educational Services created this geometry resource to help you practice geometric concepts. Please work through the practice problems and then check your work at the back of the book where the answer keys are located.

These practice worksheets should be used to supplement strong and viable curriculum that encourages differentiation for all diverse learners. They can be used at home, in tutoring sessions, or at school.

Table of Contents

Introduction to Proofs

Generally speaking, we prove things every day. Have you ever asked, "why?" You are demanding proof before you believe something. In mathematics, we need proof before we can believe something. One logical way we deduce whether something is true or not, is through proofs. A proof is an argument which contains:

1. A theorem—this is a statement which can be proven as indeed true.

2. Postulates—these are things we assume to be true without question.

3. Axioms—these are "self-evident" facts.

Example 1: Proof for the area of a triangle

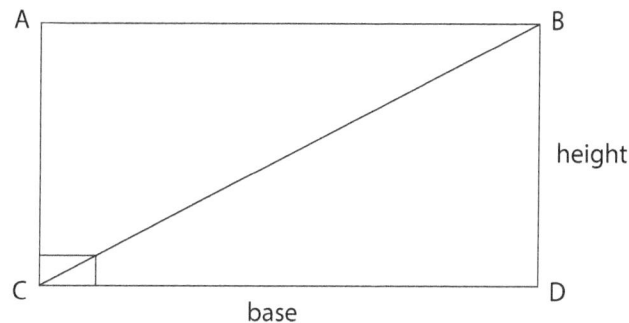

Figure 1

Begin by looking at the area of a right triangle. Simply enough, we know that the formula is, $A = \frac{1}{2}bh$, but how do we derive this? Well, we know that to find the area of a quadrilateral, in this case a rectangle, we multiply, $A = bh$. From the image we can deduce that the area of a right triangle is half of the area of a quadrilateral.

Algebraic Proofs

Chances are, you have already learned how to solve basic algebraic equations. They are easy enough, but what would happen if I asked you to prove it? It is the same reason you want to know why your parents ask you to do something. We need to know why a particular solution works. It is a good idea to familiarize yourself with basic algebraic properties, and know WHY you take certain steps.

Properties of Equality

Addition Property	If $a=b$, then $a+c=b+c$.
Subtraction Property	If $a=b$, then $a-c=b-c$.
Multiplication Property	If $a=b$, then $a \cdot c=b \cdot c$.
Division Property	If $a=b$, then $\dfrac{a}{c}=\dfrac{b}{c}$
Substitution Property	If $a=b$ then you may substitute b for any a.
Distributive Property	$a(b+c)=ab+ac$
Transitive Property	If $a=b$ and $b=c$, then $a=c$.
Reflexive Property	Where a is any real number, and $a=a$, if $a=b$, then $b=a$.

11. If $a=12$, $c=10$, and $a=b$, what does $b+c$ equal? Why?

12. If $a=4$, $c=6$, and $a=b$, what does $b=c$ equal? Why?

13. Simplify the following: $hk(3+4)+xy(2+3)$.

14. If $a=b$, and $b=5$, evaluate the following: $4a+2=?$ What property is this?

15. If you know that $(b)(c)=12$, and $(a)(c)=12$, prove that $b=a$.

16. What is a proof? Why is it useful in mathematics today? Haven't we learned all there is to no about math?

17. Can you prove that $x = 4$, if you are given the following: $3x - 10 = 2$?

18. Can you prove that $x = 6$, if you are given the following: $5x - 10 = 15$?

19. Can you prove that $x = \dfrac{1}{2}$, if you are given the following: $24x = 12$?

20. Can you prove that $x = 4$, if you are given the following: $3x + 5 = 17$?

Proofs have two basic structures. First, we typically look at two column proofs. Paragraphs proofs are simply proofs written in language. The key to writing paragraph proofs is to make certain that each step is clearly defined and reasoned. Direct proofs use deductive reasoning to make their point. This is the most common type of proof used for geometry. Indirect proofs are also important to geometry. This is the method in which we show how all the other possible options are false.

A flowchart proof is a way in which we are able to map out our proofs—statements and reasons. This helps us determine the logical order of things.

Example:

Prove that $x = \dfrac{5}{6}$, if you are given the following: $5x - 10 = 15$.

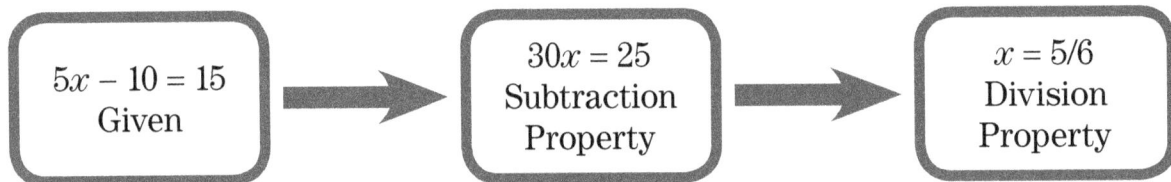

| $5x - 10 = 15$
 Given | → | $30x = 25$
 Subtraction
 Property | → | $x = 5/6$
 Division
 Property |

Prove the following: If $3x - 15 = 45$, then $x = 20$.

| | → | | → | |

Prove that $x = 4$, if you are given the following: $3x + 5 = 17$.

| | → | | → | |

Prove that $x = \dfrac{1}{2}$, if you are given the following: $24x = 12$.

$$\boxed{} \longrightarrow \boxed{} \longrightarrow \boxed{}$$

Prove that $x = 4$, if you are given the following: $3x - 10 = 2$.

$$\boxed{} \longrightarrow \boxed{} \longrightarrow \boxed{}$$

Prove that $x = 10$ if you are given $3x + 35 = 65$.

$$\boxed{} \longrightarrow \boxed{} \longrightarrow \boxed{}$$

Biconditional and Conditional Statements

We generally use bioconditional statements to create definitions. When studying logic and abstract mathematics, bioconditional statements are compound statements joined by "and." Sometimes these are known "and" statements. A biconditional statement can only be true if both components are true, or have the same truth value. These may also be denoted by "iff," which represents, "if and only if."

Example:

If we have the biconditional statement, $x = 2 \, iff \, x^2 = 4$.

We can write the conditional statement: $If \, x = 2, then \, x^2 = 4$. We can also write the converse, $If \, x^2 = 4, then \, x = 2$.

For each of the following biconditional statements write the conditional statement.

1. $n = 1$ iff $n \mid n$. "n equals one, if and only if n divides n."

2. $3n$ is even if and only if n is an even integer.

3. I will be happy if and only if it rains.

4. Spock is logical if and only if he is part Vulcan.

5. Penny is furry if and only if she is a cat.

6. Angles are perpendicular if and only if they are orthogonal.

7. $x > 2$ iff $x = 5$.

8. Circles are equal to squares if and only if cows bark.

9. x is a real number iff $x > 0$.

10. It is snowing if and only if it is Christmas.

Biconditional and Conditional Statements; Dealing With the Converse

We recall what we know about condtional statements—A conditional statement is known as an "if-then statement." A conditional statement is true if the first part is false (the "if" part), or if both parts are true. We now need to understand Converse, inverse, and contrapositive.

Example:

Let's start with a conditional statement, "If it has pointy ears, then it is an alien."

Converse	If it is an alien, then it has pointy ears.
Inverse	If it does not have pointy ears, then it is not an alien.
Contrapositive	If it is not an alien, then it does not have pointy ears.

Fill out the charts respectively.

"If it is raining, then it is cold."

Converse	
Inverse	
Contrapositive	

"If it is has a tune, then it is music."

Converse	
Inverse	

Contrapositive	

"If it is adorable, then it is a kitten."

Converse	
Inverse	
Contrapositive	

"If you fail the test, then you did not study."

Converse	
Inverse	
Contrapositive	

"If the road is yellow, then we are off to see the wizard."

Converse	
Inverse	
Contrapositive	

Midpoint and Distance in the Coordinate Plane

Recall that there is an axiom which states that between any two points, there is a line. What if we want to calculate the distance between these two points? We can use the distance formula to calculate the length of the line segment.

The distance formula, given two points (x_1, x_2), (y_1, y_2):

$$Distance = \sqrt{(x_2 - x_1)^2 + (y_2 - y_1)^2}.$$

Example: Calculate the distance between the points: $(1,2), (3,4)$.

$$Distance = \sqrt{(3-1)^2 + (4-2)^2}$$

$$D = \sqrt{2^2 + 2^2} \rightarrow \sqrt{4+4} \rightarrow \sqrt{8}.$$

For the following, draw an appropriately scaled *cartesian coordinate plane*, plot the points, then solve for the distance.

- Find the distance between the points: $(4,4),(6,6)$.

- Find the distance between the points: $(0,1),(\pi,0)$.

- Find the distance between the points: $(2\pi,1),(3\pi,5)$.

- Find the distance between the points: $(3x,y),(x,0)$. You do not have to graph these points.

- Find the distance between the points: $(x^2,y),(3x^2,2y)$. You do not have to graph these points.

Midpoint and Distance in the Coordinate Plane

Recall that there is an axiom which states that between any two points, there is a line. What if we want to calculate the distance halfway between these two points? We can use the midpoint formula to calculate the distance exactly half the length of the line segment.

The midpoint formula, given two points (x_1, x_2), (y_1, y_2):

$$Midpoint = \left(\left(\frac{x_1 + x_2}{2} \right), \left(\frac{y_1 + y_2}{2} \right) \right).$$

Example: Calculate the midpoint between the points: (1, 2), (3, 4).

$$Midpoint = \left(\left(\frac{1+3}{2} \right), \left(\frac{2+4}{2} \right) \right) \rightarrow Midpoint = \left(\frac{4}{2}, \frac{6}{2} \right) = (2, 3).$$

1. (2, 3)(5, 6)

2. (5, 11)(6, 4)

3. (2, 3)(6, 4)

4. (1, 2) (6, 7)

5. (4.6, 7.2) (5, 21)

6. (4, 2.4) (4.5, 6.23)

7. (9.01, 8.33) (3.21, 32)

8. (4.44, 2) (1.1, 3)

9. (4, 7)(7.53, 7.23)

10. (0, 1) (1, 0)

11. (1, 1) (1, 1)

12. (1, 2) (2, 1)

13. (2, 45) (88, 12)

14. (5.6, 8.44) (4.22, 11)

14. (14, 7)(7, 14)

16. (0, 5) (.5, 3)

The law of sine and cosine are both useful for solving for solving for triangles. Use the following diagram to help you interpret each law. When solving for these, be sure your calculator is set to degrees rather than radians.

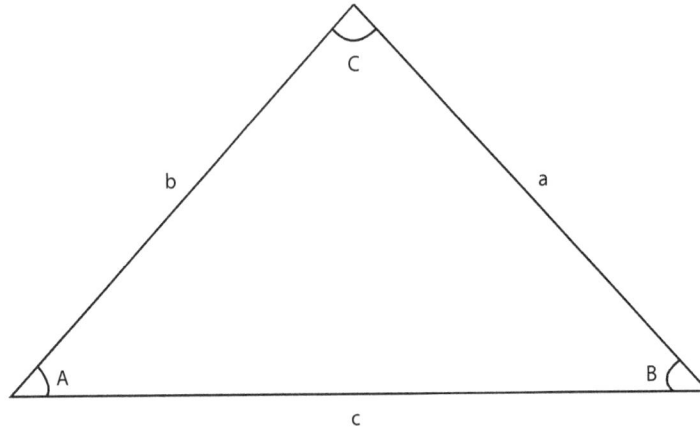

Figure 1

- The Law of Sines: $\dfrac{a}{sinA} = \dfrac{b}{sinB} = \dfrac{c}{sinC}$.

- The Law of Cosines: $c^2 = a^2 + b^2 - 2abcos(C)$.

Use *Figure 1* to solve the following using the Law of Sines:

1. $B = 80$, $C = 40$, $a = 20$

2. $A = 33$, $C = 81$, $c = 28$

3. $A = 42$, $C = 70$, $c = 36$

4. $A = 24$, $B = 61$, $c = 40$

5. $A = 30, C = 60, b = 25$

Use *Figure 1* to solve the following using the Law of Cosines:

6. $C = 115$, $a = 10$, $b = 15$

7. $B = 50$, $a = 4$, $c = 8$

8. $A = 64$, $b = 4$, $c = 5$

9. $B = 80$, $a = 2$, $c = 1$

10. $C = 77$, $a = 1$, $b = 1$

Side-Side-Side

Side-Side-Side, or SSS, is a congruence postulate which states that if the sides of a triangle are congruent to the sides of another triangle, then the two are congruent.

Example:

$$\triangle ABC \cong \triangle DEF$$

All of the sides are congruent: $\overline{FD} = \overline{CA}$, $\overline{DE} = \overline{AB}$, $\overline{EF} = \overline{BC}$.
We can conclude, according to SSS, the two triangles must be congruent.

What does it mean for two sides to be congruent?

State four observations about the following triangle:

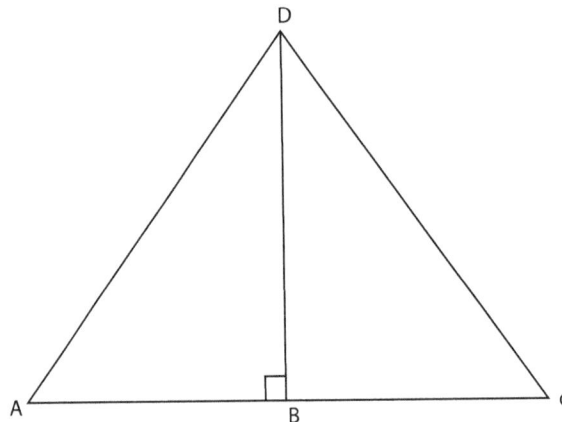

Figure 1

   1.

   2.

   3.

   4.

What conclusions can we draw from the statements above? What postulate, if any, did you use?

Two shapes are _____ if they are the same size, shape, and dimensions.

Side Angle Side

Side Angle Side, or SAS is a congruence postulate. This postulate states that if there are two sides are congruent to another triangle, and if the included angles are congruent, then the triangles are congruent.

Example:

$$\triangle ABC \cong \triangle DEF$$

We know that two sides are congruent, and the included angles are congruent: $AC = FD$, $\angle ACB = \angle DFE$, and $CB = FE$, hence, Side-Angle-Side.

We can conclude from this postulate that the two triangles are congruent.

Explain the idea of congruence.

Define the "included angle."

We now understand how to use SAS, but can we have a Angle-Side-Side postulate?

How can we use the Law of Cosines to solve for a Side-Angle-Side triangle?

How can we use the Law of Sines to solve for a Side-Angle-Side triangle?

How can we find the last angle after solving for the other two?

Please draw the included angle between two line segments:

Angle Side Angle

For the Angle Side Angle postulate, or ASA, tells us that we have the side and the two angles it is between.

Example:

$$\triangle ABC \cong \triangle DEF$$

The included side and angles are congruent: $\angle CAB = \angle FDE$, $AB = XY$, $\angle ABC = \angle XYZ$. We can conclude from ASA that both triangles are congruent.

What is the included side?

Please draw an example of an included side, also indicate any included angles.

We know that the triangles are congruent, and we are given two angles, what can we conclude about the third angles?

We know that the triangles are congruent, and we are given one of the sides, what can we conclude about the remaining sides?

True or False, Congruent triangles can be mirror images of each other, or they can be rotated.

Knowing you must use the ASA postulate, label what you would be given (the known angles, sides, etc) in the following triangle.

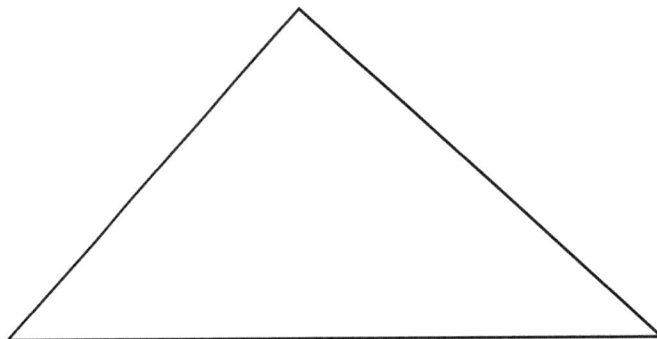

Angle-Angle-Side and Hypotenuse-Leg

The angle-angle-side postulate, or AAS tells us that we can prove two triangles are congruent if we know that two angles are equal, as well as the non-included side.

The hypotenuse-leg postulate, or HL, only applies to right triangles. This means we know one leg, the hypotenuse, and one angle (90°).

Are the following congruent? Which theorem did you use?

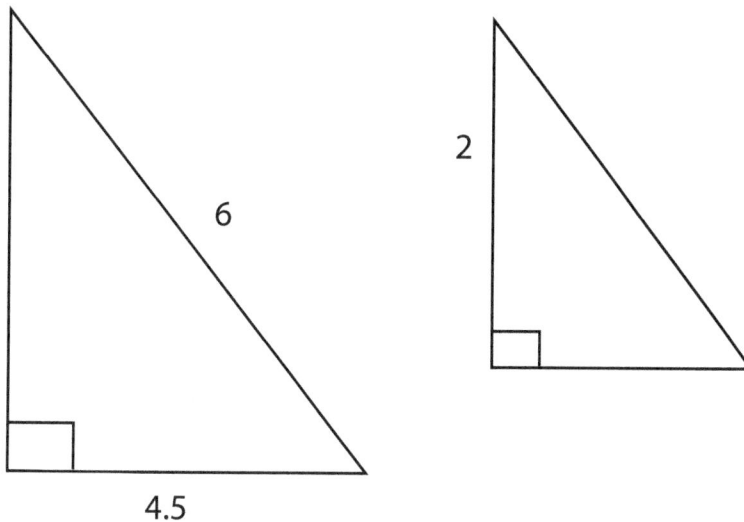

Figure 1

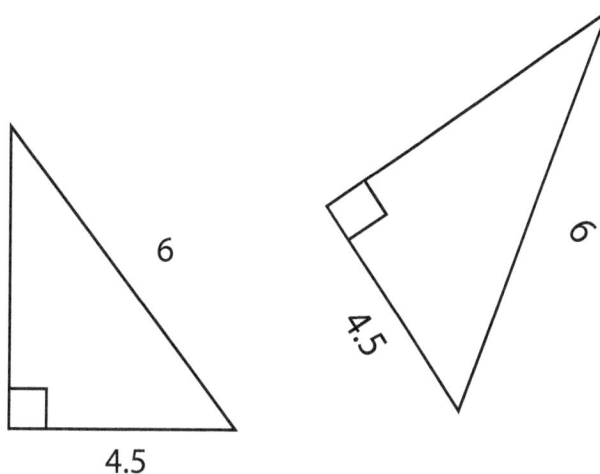

Figure 2

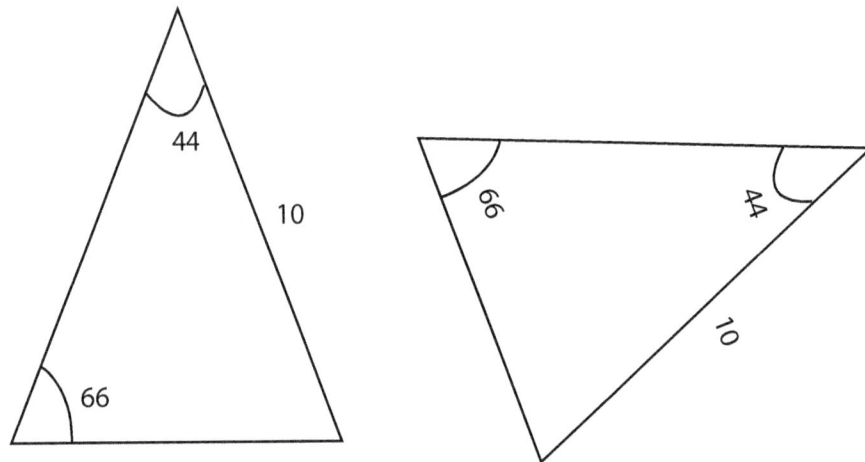

Figure 3

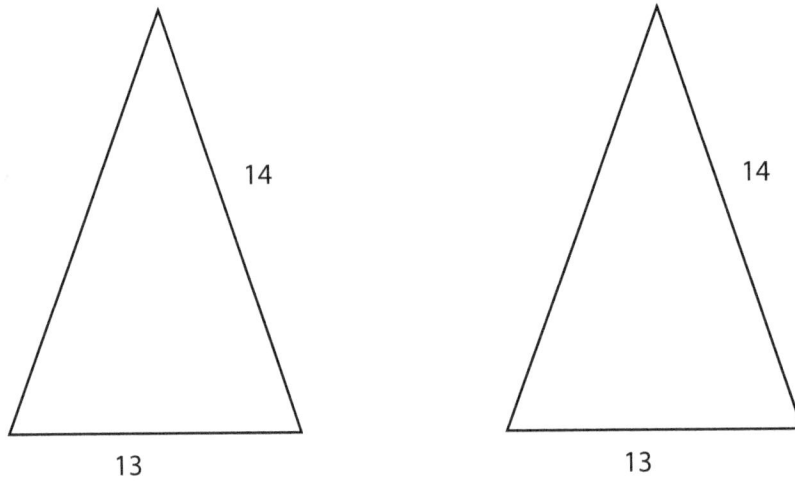

Figure 4

Vector Basics; Finding the Magnitude

A vector can be described as a line which has magnitude (The magnitude is essentially the length) and direction. This could be a vector:

You can add vectors simply by connecting them head to tail, and it is important to note that order does not matter in this case. To subtract vectors, simply reverse the direction and add as you normally. To do vectors with an arrow over the letters: $\overrightarrow{AB}$. You may also see them written in bold.

To find the magnitude of vector **a**, denoted $|a|$. The formula is: $|a| = \sqrt{x^2 + y^2 + z^2}$. Let's practice finding the magnitude:

1. <1,2>

2. <3,5>

3. <4,5>

4. <7,7>

5. <9,2>

6. <1,2,6>

7. <3,3,6>

8. <4,5,9>

9. <6,7,3>

10. <5,6,9>

Corresponding Parts of Congruent Triangles Congruent (CPCTC)

What does CPCTC stand for? Well it stands for, Corresponding Parts of Congruent Triangles Congruent. Sounds like a jumble of words doesn't it? It actually means that if we know that two triangles are congruent, then all of their respective angles and sides are congruent as well. Simple enough?

Write a relationship about the following which can be proven using CPCTC.

We know that $\triangle QRS \cong \triangle TUS$

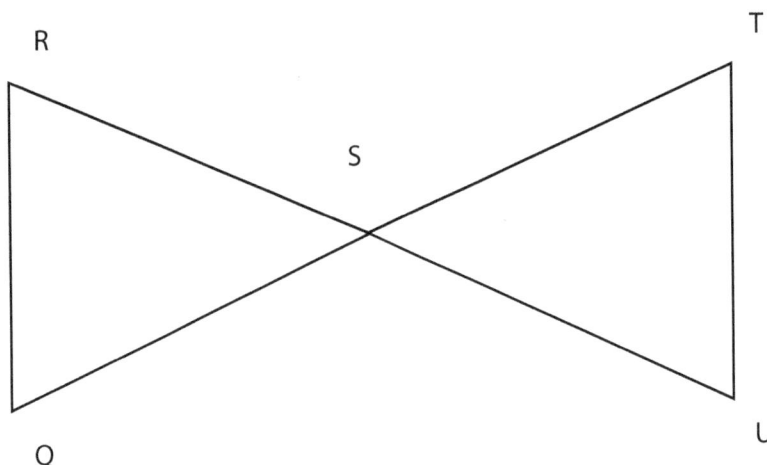

Figure 1

Use figure 1 for the following:

Write a proof the show that S represents the midpoint of RU and QT, if we know RQ and TU are parallel. Identify which step stands for the CPCTC.

Statements:

Sector Area and Arc Length

Trigonometry seems hard enough, but then we have to learn the trigonometry of circles. Beginning with arc length, we know that an arc is simply a section of the circumference of a circle. Please draw an arc:

Now, that we can identify an arc, how do we find the length of it? The formula to find the arc length in radians is: $Arc\,Length = \theta r$. To find the arc length in degrees the formula is: $Arc\,Length = \theta r \left(\dfrac{\pi}{180} \right)$.

Use figure 1 to find the arc length (in degrees) of the following:

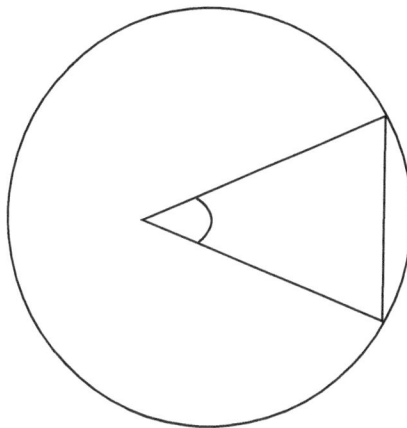

Figure 1

- Find the arc length where $r = 5$ and $\theta = 50$.

- Find the arc length where $r = 7$ and $\theta = 66$.

- Find the arc length where $r = 10$ and $\theta = 76$.

- Find the arc length where $r = 7$ and $\theta = 66$.

- Find the arc length where $r = 12$ and $\theta = 88$.

- Find the arc length where $r = 7$ and $\theta = 40$.

The sector of a circle can be thought of like a piece of the pie. Try drawing and shading in a sector of a circle:

To find the sector of the circle in radians, use the formula: $Sector\ Area = \dfrac{\theta}{2}r^2$. To find the area in degrees: $Sector\ Area = \dfrac{\theta}{360}\pi r^2$.

Use figure 1 to find the sector area (in degrees) for the following:

- Find the arc length where $r = 5$ and $\theta = 50$.

- Find the arc length where $r = 7$ and $\theta = 66$.

- Find the arc length where $r = 10$ and $\theta = 76$. $r = 10 \, and \, \theta = 76$.

- Find the arc length where $r = 7$ and $\theta = 66$.

- Find the arc length where $r = 12$ and $\theta = 88$.

- Find the arc length where $r = 7$ and $\theta = 40$.

Arcs and Chords; Finding Chord Length

A chord is a line segment which contains only part of the circle. The diameter is a chord which is through the dead center of the circle. How do we calculate the length of a chord? We calculate the length depending on what we are provided.

- If you are given the central angle and the radius:

$$chord\,length = 2r sin\left(\frac{c}{2}\right)$$

- If you are given the distance to the center and the radius:

$$chord\,length = 2\sqrt{r^2 - d^2}$$

1. $c = 60°$ and $r = 6$

2. $r = 5$ and $d = 6$

3. $r = 3$ and $d = 4$

4. $c = 40°$ and $r = 5$

5. $r = 3$ and $d = 5$

6. $r = 5$ and $r = 7$

7. $r = 8$ and $d = 7$

8. $c = 66°$ and $r = 5$

9. $c = 75°$ and $r = 4$

10. $c = 54°$ and $r = 5$

Composite Figures

Composite figures are those shapes which appear to be made of two or more shapes. Try drawing a composite figure... you could draw a house, an arrow, a space ship. You could drajust about anything.

For the following divide the composite shape into its two parts:

Figure 1

How do we find the area of a composite figure? Simply divide the shape into its respective shapes, calculate the area of each, then sum those individual areas together.

Find the area of the following composite figures:

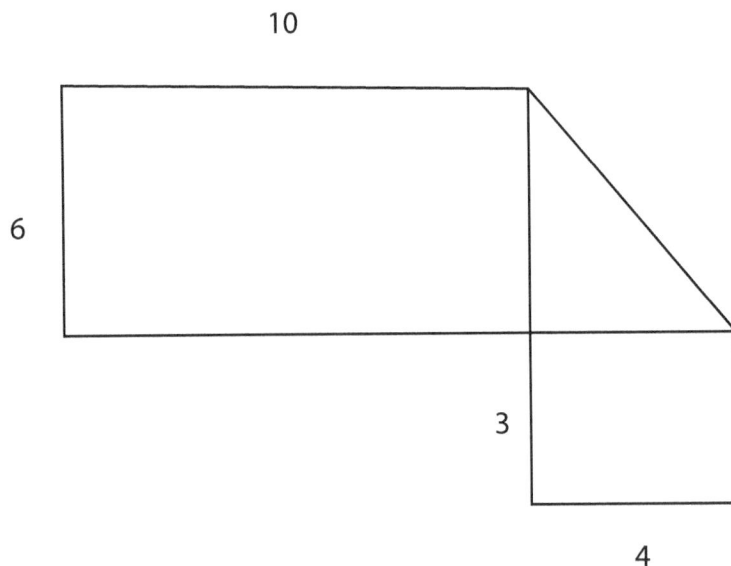

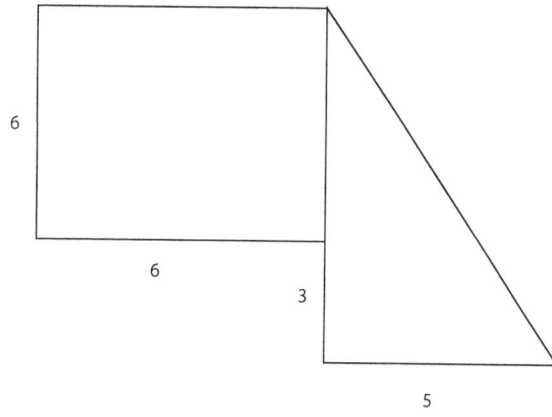

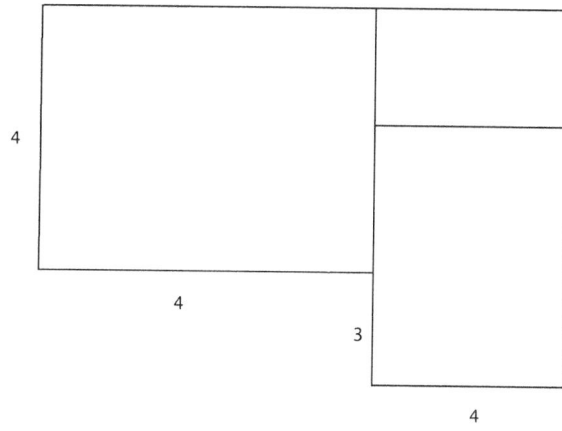

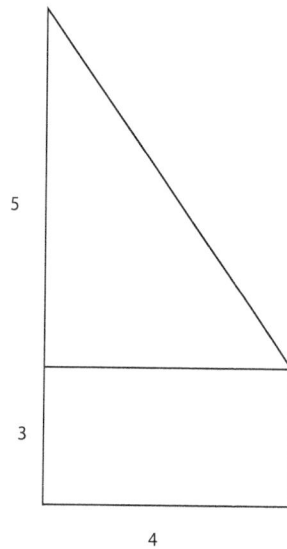

The Axiomatic Systems of Geometry

What is an Axiom, or an axiomatic statement? An axiomatic statement is one which is just evidently true. We may also refer to an axiom as a postulate. A theorem is perhaps the most important part of an axiomatic system as it contains the respective proofs. Proofs are the way in which we are able to logically deduce an argument, or a set of premises.

In these systems there are, in fact, some terms which are defined and some which are not. Euclid himself made the attempt to define each and every term, however, we now accept that this is an impossible task.

Please give an example of an undefined term:

What do you think a perfect axiomatic system might contain?

In **Euclidean geometry** what sort of method is used to prove various theorems?

What does it mean to use a constructive proof?

Discuss and Define *Point, Line and Plane.*

Fill in the blank:

.............................will go on infinitely without ever touching or intersecting.

.... intersect so that a 90 degree angle is formed at the point of intersection.

Just remember, in order to solve ANY problem in trigonometry, you must only understand these four concepts:

1. Be able to understand the components of a right triangle.

2. Use the given angles to find the respective lengths of sides.

3. The hypotenuse represents the total displacement of distance.

4. Understand how to write and solve for equations with a single variable.

The Distance Formula

Recall that there is an axiom which states that between any two points, there is a line. What if we want to calculate the distance between these two points? We can use the distance formula to calculate the length of the line segment.

The distance formula, given two points (x_1, x_2), (y_1, y_2):

$$Distance = \sqrt{(x_2 - x_1)^2 + (y_2 - y_1)^2}.$$

1. $(2, 7), (8, 9)$

2. $(4, 7), (6, 3)$

3. $(1, 8), (5, 3)$

4. $(3, 5), (7, 1)$

5. $(5, 5), (4, 4)$

6. $(3, 4), (4, 5)$

7. $(8, 6), (11, 3)$

8. (3, 7), (15, 7)

9. (12, 5), (4, 15)

10. (17, 9), (6, 11)

The Midpoint Formula

Recall that there is an axiom which states that between any two points, there is a line. What if we want to calculate the distance halfway between these two points? We can use the midpoint formula to calculate the distance exactly half the length of the line segment.

The midpoint formula, given two points $(x_1, x_2), (y_1, y_2)$:

$$Midpoint = \left(\left(\frac{x_1 + x_2}{2} \right), \left(\frac{y_1 + y_2}{2} \right) \right).$$

1. $(2, 7), (8, 9)$

2. $(4, 7), (6, 3)$

3. $(1, 8), (5, 3)$

4. $(3, 5), (7, 1)$

5. $(5, 5), (4, 4)$

6. $(3, 4), (4, 5)$

7. $(8, 6), (11, 3)$

8. (3, 7), (15, 7)

9. (12, 5), (4, 15)

10. (17, 9), (6, 11)

Cartesian Coordinate Plane; Practicing Plots

(0,5), (1,6), (2,7), (3,8), (4,8), (5,8), (6,8), (7,8), (7,5), (7,3), (6,1), (5,0), (4,–1), (3,–2), (2,–3), (1,–4), (0,–5), (–1,–4), (–2,–3), (–3,–2), (–4,–1), (–5,0), (–6,1), (–7,3), (–7,5), (–7,8) (–6,8), (–5,8), (–4,8), (–3,8), (–2,7), (–1,6)

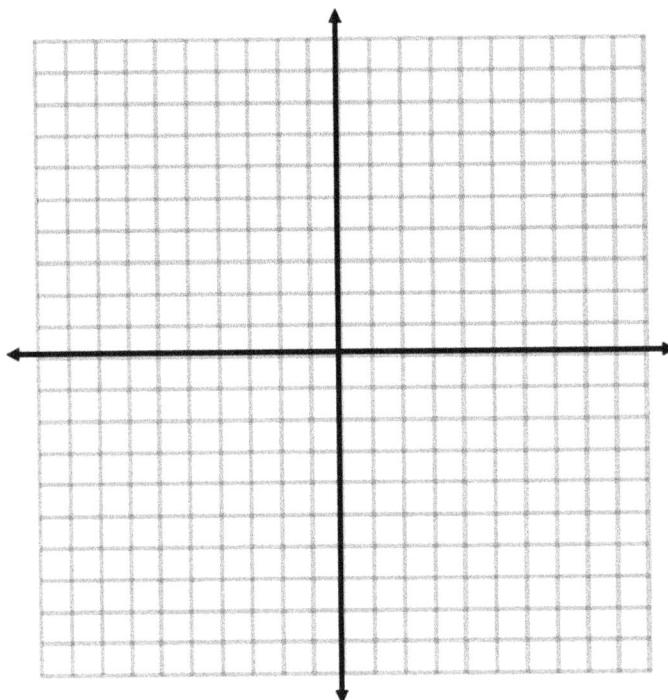

Inverse Trigonometric Ratios

By now we know how to find $\sin(x)$, $\cos(x)$ or $\tan(x)$ How do we find something of the form $a = \sin(x)$? The answer is much simpler than you would think! We simply use inverse trigonometric ratios, in the form $\sin^{-1}(a)$.

We call these the following:

$\sin^{-1}$	*arcsine*
$\cos^{-1}$	*arccosine*
$\tan^{-1}$	*arctangent*

1. $\sin(x) = .482$

2. $\sin(x) = .551$

3. $\cos(x) = .774$

4. $\tan(x) = .88$

5. $\tan(x) = .562$

6. $\cos(x) = .542$

7. $\sin(x) = .321$

8. $\sin(x) = .213$

9. $\cos(x) = .564$

10. $\tan(x) = .977$

Practice Workbook
Answer Keys

Introduction to Proofs

Question 1:

Now it is your turn, use the image below to prove the area of a scalene triangle. Label the height in the drawing, as well as the vertex and sides.

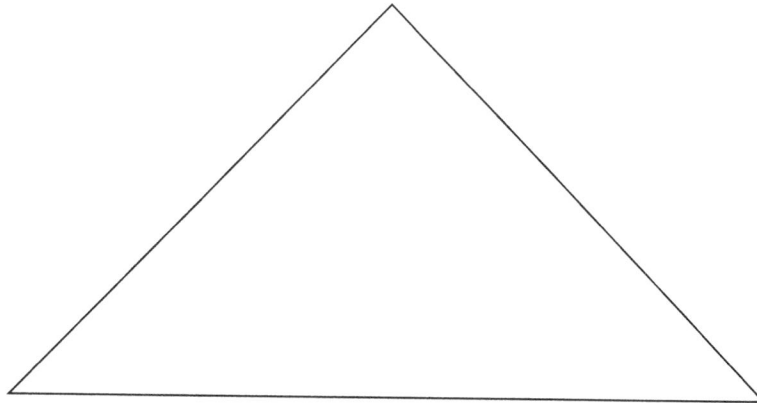

Figure 2

Proof:

vertex

height

base 1   base 2

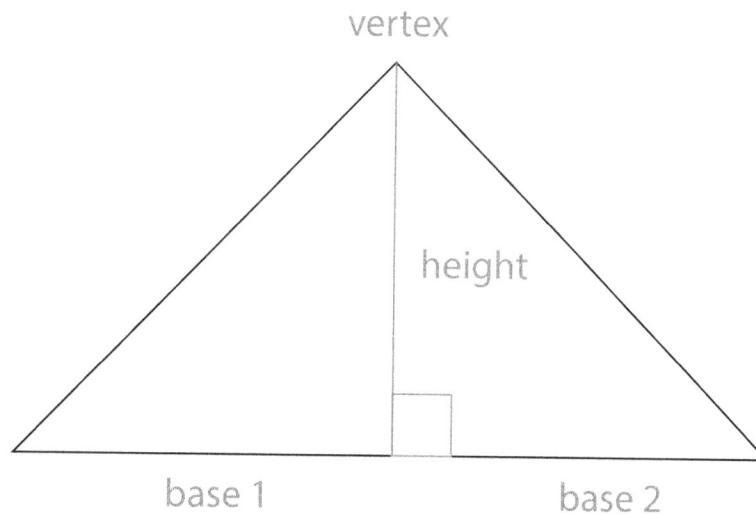

The triangle is divided into two right triangles, so we can deduce that the area of the triangle is: $Area = \frac{base1(height)}{2} + \frac{base2(height)}{2} \rightarrow (base1)(height) + \frac{base2(height)}{2} \rightarrow height(base1 + base2)$, we now take note, that $base1 + base2 = b$, therefore, $Area = (height)(base)/2$.

Since we now understand that proofs are simply logical arguments for something, we need to move on to a more formal way of doing proofs. This is where the two column proof comes in.

Example 2: Two column proofs

1. Given that: $\overline{AC} \cong \overline{DB}$ & $\overline{AB} \cong \overline{DC}$, prove that $\triangle ABC \cong \triangle DBC$.

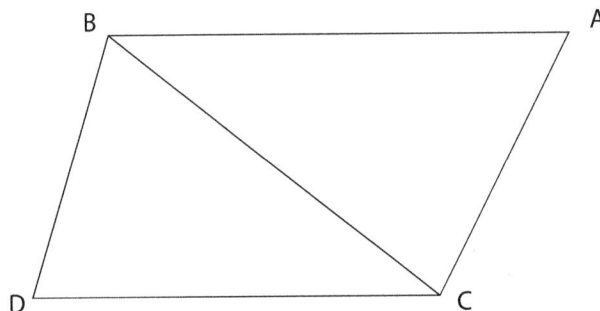

Figure 3

Statement	Reason
$\overline{AC} \cong \overline{DB}$	Given to us
$\overline{AB} \cong \overline{DC}$	Given to us
$\overline{BC} \cong \overline{BC}$	Use Reflexive Property
$\triangle ABC \cong \triangle DBC$	Side-Side-Side

Please answer the following:

2. Prove, $\triangle ABD \cong \triangle ACD$, given that $\overline{AB} \cong \overline{AC}$, and $\overline{AD}$ bisects $\overline{BC}$, knowing that D represents the height.

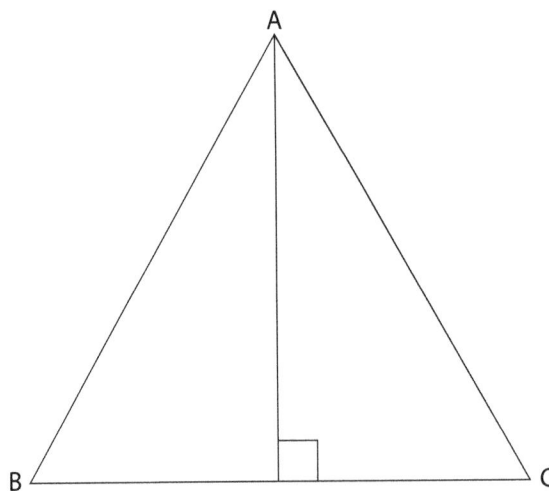

Statement	Reason
$\overline{AB} \cong \overline{AC}$	Given to us
$\overline{AD}$ bisects $\overline{BC}$	Given to us
D is the midpoint of $\overline{BC}$	D serves as a midpoint, or bisector.
$\overline{AD} \cong \overline{AD}$	Use Reflexive property
$\triangle ABD \cong \triangle ACD$	Side-Side-Side

It is important in understanding abstract mathematics, to understand what exactly a statement is. For questions 4–7 identify whether these are statements or otherwise.

4. Today is a fantastic day. Statement.

5. Go run a mile. Not a statement.

6. The Pythagorean Theorem: $a^2 + b^2 = c^2$. Not a statement.

7. $5 < 2$. Statement.

8. The Pythagorean Theorem is perhaps one of the most well-known theorems. Why do we call this a theorem rather than say, a hypothesis?

   This can be proven to be true.

9. What is the following an example of, "Any two points may be connected by a straight line?"

   This is one of Euclid's Postulates

10. Name the three steps or parts in a valid argument.

Hypothesis
Premises
Conclusion

Algebraic Proofs

Chances are, you have already learned how to solve basic algebraic equations. They are easy enough, but what would happen if I asked you to prove it? It is the same reason you want to know why your parents ask you to do something. We need to know why a particular solution works. It is a good idea to familiarize yourself with basic algebraic properties, and know WHY you take certain steps.

Properties of Equality

Addition Property	$If\ a=b, then\ a+c=b+c.$
Subtraction Property	$If\ a=b, then\ a-c=b-c.$
Multiplication Property	$If\ a=b, then\ a\cdot c=b\cdot c.$
Division Property	$If\ a=b, then\ \dfrac{a}{c}=\dfrac{b}{c}.$
Substitution Property	$If\ a=b, then\ you\ may\ substitute\ b\ for\ aqny\ a.$
Distributive Property	$a(b+c)=ab+ac$
Transitive Property	$If\ a=b\ and\ b=c, then\ a=c.$
Reflexive Property	$Where\ a\ is\ any\ real\ number, and\ a=a, if\ a=b, then\ b=a.$

1. If $a=12$, $c=10$, and $a=b$, what does $b+c$ equal? Why?

$a+c=22$, therefore we know $b+c=22$. Addition Property.

2. If $a=4$, $c=6$, and $a=b$, what does $b=c$ equal? Why?

$a*c=24$, therefore we use the multiplication property.

3. Simplify the following: $hk(3+4)+xy(2+3)$.

$$3hk+4hk+2xy+3xy$$

Combine like terms: $7hk+5xy$

4. If $a=b$, and $b=5$, evaluate the following: $4a+2=?$ What property is this?

$4(5)+2=22$; Substitution.

5. If you know that $(b)(c)=12$, and $(a)(c)=12$, prove that $b=a$.

Consider the multiplication property, and make any number of logical deductions. This is abstract thinking.

6. What is a proof? Why is it useful in mathematics today? Haven't we learned all there is to no about math?

We are still discovering "new math" every day. Arguably, calculus wasn't completed until the 1970's. A proof is how we make logical deduction when doing research in mathematics or using it in any number of fields.

7. Can you prove that $x = 4$, if you are given the following: $3x - 10 = 2$?

Two methods.

1. Evaluate: $3(4) - 10 = 2$.

2. Solve for $x : 3x - 10 = 2 \rightarrow 3x = 12 \rightarrow x = 4$.

8. Can you prove that $x = 6$, if you are given the following: $5x - 10 = 15$?

Solve for $x : 5x - 10 = 15 \rightarrow 30x = 25 \rightarrow x = \dfrac{5}{6}$. This cannot be proven.

9. Can you prove that $x = \dfrac{1}{2}$, if you are given the following: $24x = 12$?

Solve for $x : 24x = 12 \rightarrow x = \dfrac{12}{24} \rightarrow Simplify : x = \dfrac{1}{2}$.

10. Can you prove that $x = 4$, if you are given the following: $3x + 5 = 17$?

$3x + 5 = 17 \rightarrow 3x = 12 \rightarrow x = 4$.

Paragraph & Flowchart Proofs

Proofs have two basic structures. First, we typically look at two column proofs. Paravgraphs proofs are simply proofs written in language. The key to writing paragraph proofs is to make certain that each step is clearly defined and reasoned. Direct proofs use deductive reasoning to make their point. This is the most common type of proof used for geometry. Indirect proofs are also important to geometry. This is the method in which we show how all the other possible options are false.

A flowchart proof is a way in which we are able to map out our proofs—statements and reasons. This helps us determine the logical order of things.

Example:

Prove that $x = \dfrac{5}{6}$, if you are given the following: $5x - 10 = 15$.

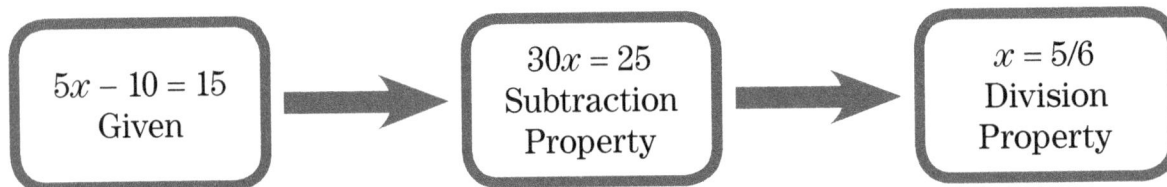

$5x - 10 = 15$ Given	→	$30x = 25$ Subtraction Property	→	$x = 5/6$ Division Property

Prove the following: If $3x - 15 = 45$, then $x = 20$.

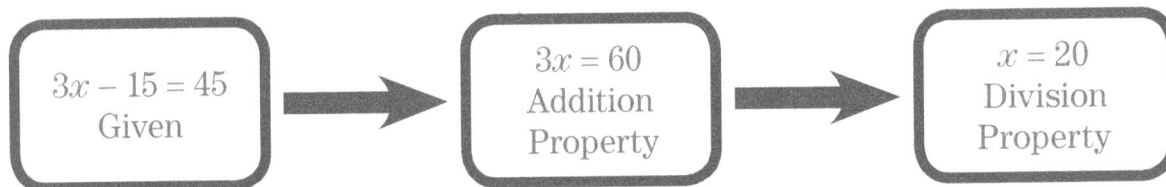

$3x - 15 = 45$ Given	→	$3x = 60$ Addition Property	→	$x = 20$ Division Property

Prove that $x = 4$, if you are given the following: $3x + 5 = 17$.

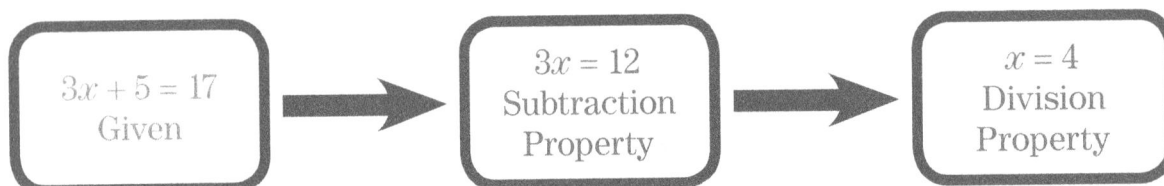

$3x + 5 = 17$ Given	→	$3x = 12$ Subtraction Property	→	$x = 4$ Division Property

Prove that $x = \dfrac{1}{2}$, if you are given the following: $24x = 12$.

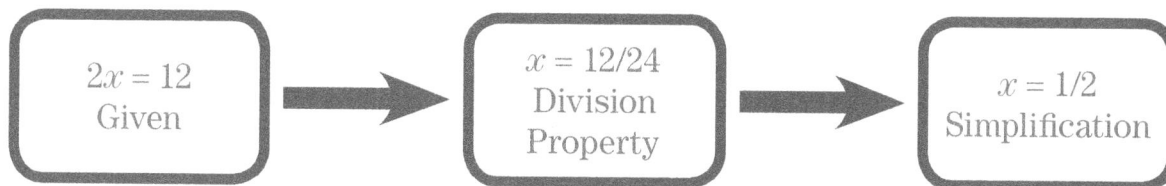

| 2x = 12
Given | → | x = 12/24
Division
Property | → | x = 1/2
Simplification |

Prove that $x = 4$, if you are given the following: $3x - 10 = 2$.

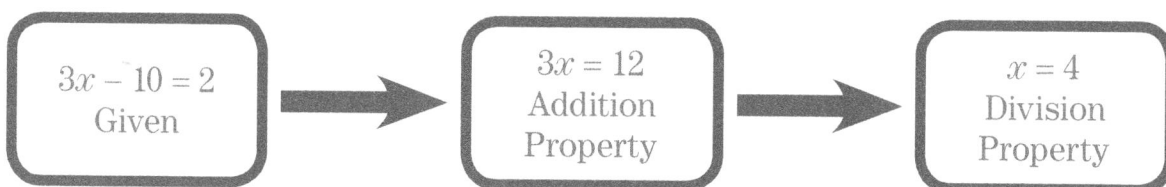

| 3x − 10 = 2
Given | → | 3x = 12
Addition
Property | → | x = 4
Division
Property |

Prove that $x = 10$ if you are given $3x + 35 = 65$.

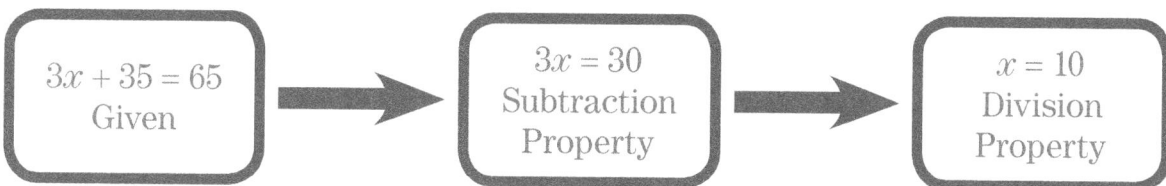

| 3x + 35 = 65
Given | → | 3x = 30
Subtraction
Property | → | x = 10
Division
Property |

Biconditional and Conditional Statements

We generally use bioconditional statements to create definitions. When studying logic and abstract mathematics, bioconditional statements are compound statements joined by "and." Sometimes these are known "and" statements. A biconditional statement can only be true if both components are true, or have the same truth value. These may also be denoted by "iff," which represents, "if and only if."

A conditional statement is known as an "if-then statement." A conditional statement is true if the first part is false (the "if" part), or if both parts are true.

Example:

If we have the biconditional statement, $x = 2\ iff\ x^2 = 4$.

We can write the conditional statement: *If $x = 2, then\ x^2 = 4$*. We can also write the converse, *If $x^2 = 4, then\ x = 2$.*

For each of the following biconditional statements write the conditional statement.

1. $n = 1$ iff $n \mid n$. "n equals one, if and only if n divides n."

If $n = 1$, then $n \mid n$.

2. $3n$ is even if and only if n is an even integer.

If $3n$ is even, then n is an even integer.

3. I will be happy if and only if it rains.

If it rains, then I will be happy.

4. Spock is logical if and only if he is part Vulcan.

If Spock is logical, then he is part Vulcan.

5. Penny is furry if and only if she is a cat.

If Penny is furry, then she is a cat.

6. Angles are perpendicular if and only if they are orthogonal.

If angles are perpendicular, then they are orthogonal.

7. $x > 2$ iff $x = 5$.

If $x > 2$ iff $x = 5$.

8. Circles are equal to squares if and only if cows bark.

If circles are equal to squares, then cows bark.

9. x is a real number iff $x > 0$.

If x is a real number, then $x > 0$.

10. It is snowing if and only if it is Christmas.

If it snows, then it is Christmas.

Biconditional and Conditional Statements; Dealing With the Converse

We recall what we know about condtional statements—A conditional statement is known as an "if-then statement." A conditional statement is true if the first part is false (the "if" part), or if both parts are true. We now need to understand Converse, inverse, and contrapositive.

Example:

Let's start with a conditional statement, "If it has pointy ears, then it is an alien."

Converse	If it is an alien, then it has pointy ears.
Inverse	If it does not have pointy ears, then it is not an alien.
Contrapositive	If it is not an alien, then it does not have pointy ears.

Fill out the charts respectively.

"If it is raining, then it is cold."

Converse	If it is cold, then it is raining.
Inverse	If it is not raining, then it is not cold.
Contrapositive	If it is not cold, then it is not raining.

"If it is has a tune, then it is music."

Converse	If it is music, then it has a tune.
Inverse	If it does not have a tune, then it is not music.
Contrapositive	If it is not music, then it does not have a tune.

"If it is adorable, then it is a kitten."

Converse	If it is a kitten, then it is adorable.
Inverse	If it is not adorable, then it is not a kitten.
Contrapositive	If it is not a kitten, then it is not adorable.

"If you fail the test, then you did not study."

Converse	If you did not study, then you fail the test.
Inverse	If you pass the test, then you studied.
Contrapositive	If you studied, then you passed the test.

"If the road is yellow, then we are off to see the wizard."

Converse	If we are off to see the wizard, then the road is yellow.
Inverse	If the road is not yellow, then we are not going to see the wizard.
Contrapositive	If we are not going to see the wizard, then the road is not yellow.

Midpoint and Distance in the Coordinate Plane

Recall that there is an axiom which states that between any two points, there is a line. What if we want to calculate the distance between these two points? We can use the distance formula to calculate the length of the line segment.

The distance formula, given two points (x_1, x_2), (y_1, y_2):

$$Distance = \sqrt{(x_2 - x_1)^2 + (y_2 - y_1)^2} \; .$$

Example: Calculate the distance between the points: $(1,2), (3,4)$.

$$Distance = \sqrt{(3-1)^2 + (4-2)^2}$$
$$D = \sqrt{2^2 + 2^2} \rightarrow \sqrt{4+4} \rightarrow \sqrt{8} \; .$$

For the following, draw an appropriately scaled *cartesian coordinate plane*, plot the points, then solve for the distance.

- Find the distance between the points: (4, 4), (6, 6).

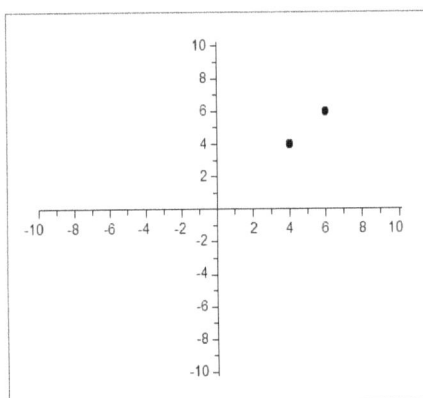

$$Distance = \sqrt{(2)^2 + (2)^2} \rightarrow \sqrt{8}$$

- Find the distance between the points: (0, 1), (π, 0).

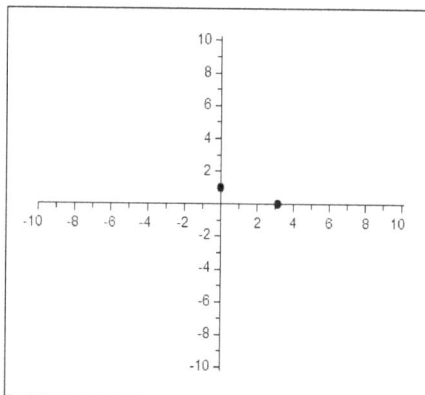

$$Distance = \sqrt{\left(\pi\right)^2 + \left(1\right)^2} = \pi.$$

- Find the distance between the points: (2π, 1), (3π, 5).

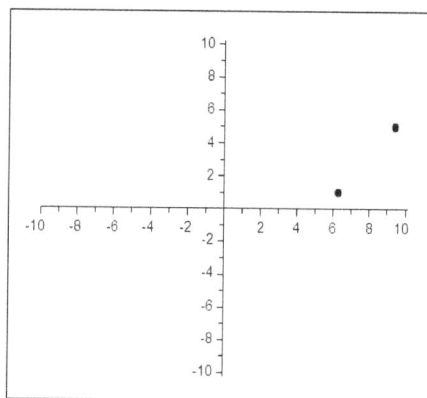

$$Distance = \sqrt{\left(\pi\right)^2 + \left(4\right)^2} = \sqrt{\pi^2 + 16} = \pi + 4$$

- Find the distance between the points: $\left(3x, y\right), \left(x, 0\right)$. You do not have to graph these points.

$$Distance = \sqrt{\left(2x\right)^2 - \left(y\right)^2} = 2x - y.$$

- Find the distance between the points: $\left(x^2, y\right), \left(3x^2, 2y\right)$. You do not have to graph these points.

$$Distance = \sqrt{\left(2x^2\right)^2 - \left(y\right)^2} = \sqrt{4x^4 - y^2} = 2x^2 - y.$$

Midpoint and Distance in the Coordinate Plane

Recall that there is an axiom which states that between any two points, there is a line. What if we want to calculate the distance halfway between these two points? We can use the midpoint formula to calculate the distance exactly half the length of the line segment.

The midpoint formula, given two points (x_1, x_2), (y_1, y_2):

$$Midpoint = \left(\left(\frac{x_1 + x_2}{2}\right), \left(\frac{y_1 + y_2}{2}\right)\right)$$

Example: Calculate the midpoint between the points: (1, 2), (3, 4).

$$Midpoint = \left(\left(\frac{1+3}{2}\right), \left(\frac{2+4}{2}\right)\right) \rightarrow Midpoint = \left(\frac{4}{2}, \frac{6}{2}\right) = (2,3).$$

1. (2, 3)(5, 6)   (3.5, 4.5)

2. (5, 11)(6, 4)   (5.5, 7.5)

3. (2, 3)(6, 4)   (4, 3.5)

4. (1, 2) (6, 7)   (3.5, 4. 5)

5. (4.6, 7.2) (5, 21)   (4.8, 14.000)

6. (4, 2.4) (4.5, 6.23)   (4.25, 4.315)

7. (9.01, 8.33) (3.21, 32)   (6.1099, 20, 165)

8. (4.44, 2) (1.1, 3)   (2.770, 2.5)

9. (4, 7)(7.53, 7.23)   (5.765, 7.115)

10. (0, 1) (1, 0)   (.5, .5)

11. (1, 1) (1, 1)   (1, 1)

12. (1, 2) (2, 1)   (1.5, 1.5)

13. (2, 45) (88, 12)   (45, 28.5)

14. (5.6, 8.44) (4.22, 11)   (4.91, 9.719)

14. (14, 7)(7, 14)   (10.5, 10.5)

16. (0, 5) (.5, 3)   (.25, 4)

Law of Sines and Cosines

The law of sine and cosine are both useful for solving for solving for triangles. Use the following diagram to help you interpret each law. When solving for these, be sure your calculator is set to degrees rather than radians.

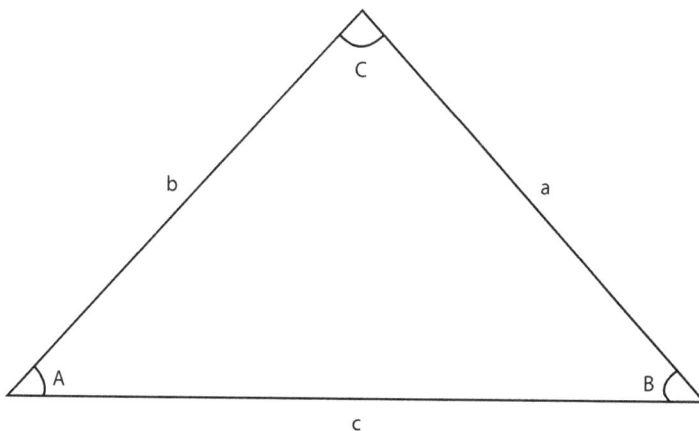

Figure 1

- The Law of Sines: $\dfrac{a}{sinA} = \dfrac{b}{sinB} = \dfrac{c}{sinC}$.

- The Law of Cosines: $c^2 = a^2 + b^2 - 2abcos(C)$.

Use *Figure 1* to solve the following using the Law of Sines:

1. $B = 80$, $C = 40$, $a = 20$

$A = 180 - (80 + 40) = 60, \ b = \dfrac{20}{sin60}(sin80), \ c = \dfrac{20}{sin60}(sin40)$

2. $A = 33$, $C = 81$, $c = 28$

$B = 180 - (33 + 81), \ a = \dfrac{28}{sin81}(\sin 33), \ b = \dfrac{15.439}{sin33}(sin66)$

3. $A = 42$, $C = 70$, $c = 36$

$B = 180 - (42 + 70), \ a = \dfrac{36}{sin70}(sin42), \ b = \dfrac{25.635}{sin42}(sin68)$

4. $A = 24$, $B = 61$, $c = 40$

$C = 180 - (24 + 61), \ a = \dfrac{40}{sin95}(sin24), \ b = \dfrac{16.3316}{sin24}(sin61)$

5. $A = 30, C = 60, b = 25$

$$B = 180 - (30 + 60), \quad a = \frac{25}{\sin 90}(sin30), \quad c = \frac{12.5}{\sin 30}(sin60) \quad c = \frac{20}{\sin 60}(sin40)$$

Use *Figure 1* to solve the following using the Law of Cosines:

6. $C = 115, a = 10, b = 15$

$$c = \sqrt{10^2 + 15^2 - (2)(10)cos115}, \quad A = cos^{-1}\left(\frac{15^2 + 21.255^2 - 10^2}{(2)(15)(21.255)}\right), \quad B = 180 - (25.239 + 115)$$

7. $B = 50, a = 4, c = 8$

$$b = \sqrt{4^2 + 8^2 - (2)(4)(8)cos50}, \quad A = \frac{cos^{-1}\left(6.2339 + 8^2 - 4^2\right)}{(2)(6.2339)(8)}, \quad C = 180 - (29.44 + 50)$$

8. $A = 64, b = 4, c = 5$

$$a = \sqrt{4^2 + 5^2 - (2)(4)(5)cos64}, \quad B = cos^{-1}\left(\frac{5^2 + 4.84 - 4^2}{(2)(5)(4.84)}\right), \quad C = 180 - (64 + 47.917)$$

9. $B = 80, a = 2, c = 1$

$$b = \sqrt{2^2 + 1 - (2)(2)(1)cos80}, \quad A = cos^{-1}\frac{2.075^2 + 1 - 2^2}{(2)(2.075)(1)}, \quad C = 180 - (71.6655 + 80)$$

10. $C = 77, a = 1, b = 1$

$$c = \sqrt{1 + 1 - 2(1*1)cos77}, \quad A = cos^{-1}\left(\frac{1 + 1.25^2 - 1}{2*1*1.245}\right), \quad B = 180 - (51.5 + 77)$$

Side-Side-Side

Side-Side-Side, or SSS, is a congruence postulate which states that if the sides of a triangle are congruent to the sides of another triangle, then the two are congruent.

Example:

$$\triangle ABC \cong \triangle DEF$$

All of the sides are congruent: $\overline{FD} = \overline{CA}$, $\overline{DE} = \overline{AB}$, $\overline{EF} = \overline{BC}$.
We can conclude, according to SSS, the two triangles must be congruent.

What does it mean for two sides to be congruent?

Identical, superimposed

State four observations about the following triangle:

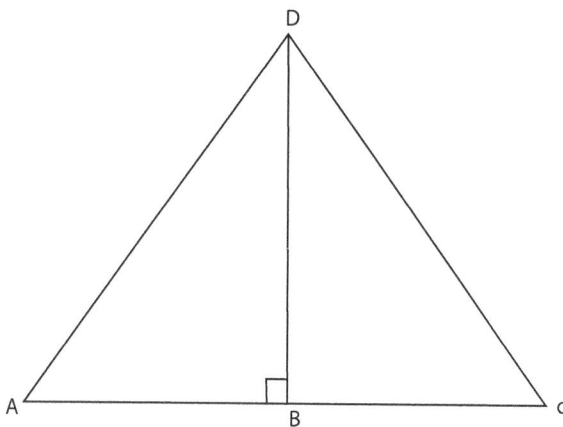

Figure 1

1. $DB \cong DB$

2. $AD \cong DC$

3. DB is the median

4. $\triangle ADB \cong \triangle CDB$

What conclusions can we draw from the statements above? What postulate, if any, did you use?

The two triangles are congruent according to SSS.

Two shapes are congruent if they are the same size, shape, and dimensions.

Side Angle Side

Side Angle Side, or SAS is a congruence postulate. This postulate states that if there are two sides are congruent to another triangle, and if the included angles are congruent, then the triangles are congruent.

Example:

$$\triangle ABC \cong \triangle DEF$$

We know that two sides are congruent, and the included angles are congruent: $AC = FD$, $\angle ACB = \angle DFE$, and $CB = FE$, hence, Side-Angle-Side.

We can conclude from this postulate that the two triangles are congruent.

Explain the idea of congruence.

Identical, superimposed. Two shapes are congruent if they are the same size, shape, and dimensions.

Define the "included angle."

When two line segments meet at the vertex, the space in between will be called the included angle. This helps us understand vectors, which are defined by the direction and magnitude.

We now understand how to use SAS, but can we have a Angle-Side-Side postulate?

This is not possible, as two sides and an angle cannot prove congruence.

How can we use the Law of Cosines to solve for a Side-Angle-Side triangle?

To calculate the third side.

How can we use the Law of Sines to solve for a Side-Angle-Side triangle?

To find one of the other angles (not the included angle).

How can we find the last angle after solving for the other two?

Add those angles together and subtract from the given 180 degrees.

Please draw the included angle between two line segments:

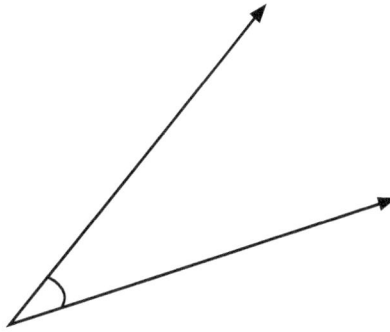

For the Angle Side Angle postulate, or ASA, tells us that we have the side and the two angles it is between.

Example:

$$\triangle ABC \cong \triangle DEF$$

The included side and angles are congruent: $\angle CAB = \angle FDE$, $AB = XY$, $\angle ABC = \angle XYZ$. We can conclude from ASA that both triangles are congruent.

What is the included side?

The included side is the common side or leg between two angles in a polygon.

Please draw an example of an included side, also indicate any included angles.

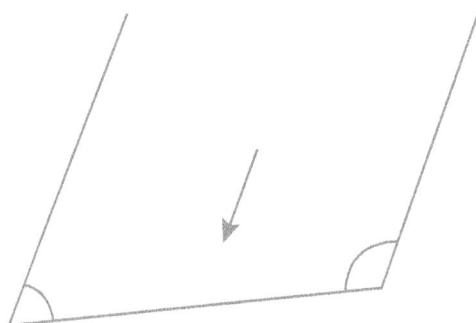

We know that the triangles are congruent, and we are given two angles, what can we conclude about the third angles?

These angles are also equal.

We know that the triangles are congruent, and we are given one of the sides, what can we conclude about the remaining sides?

The remaining sides are also equal.

True or False, Congruent triangles can be mirror images of each other, or they can be rotated.

True.

Knowing you must use the ASA postulate, label what you would be given (the known angles, sides, etc) in the following triangle.

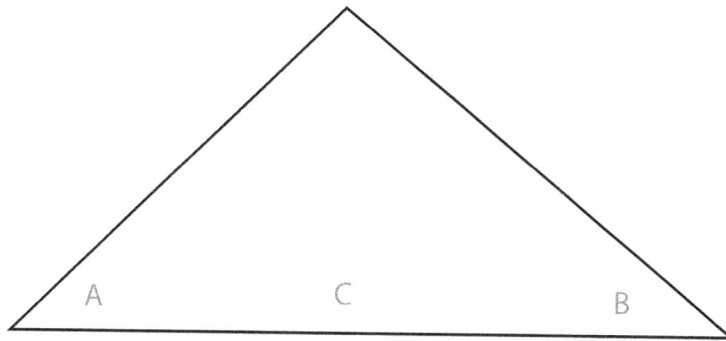

The angle-angle-side postulate, or AAS tells us that we can prove two triangles are congruent if we know that two angles are equal, as well as the non-included side.

The hypotenuse-leg postulate, or HL, only applies to right triangles. This means we know one leg, the hypotenuse, and one angle (90°).

Are the following congruent? Which theorem did you use?

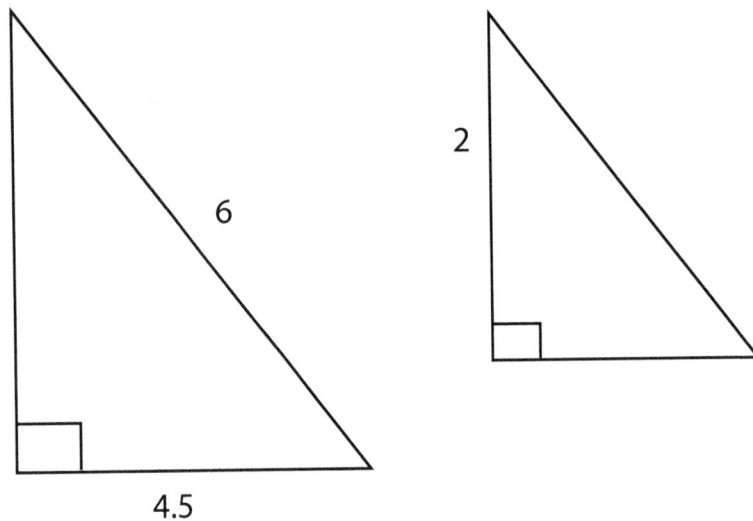

Figure 1

They are not congruent. HL

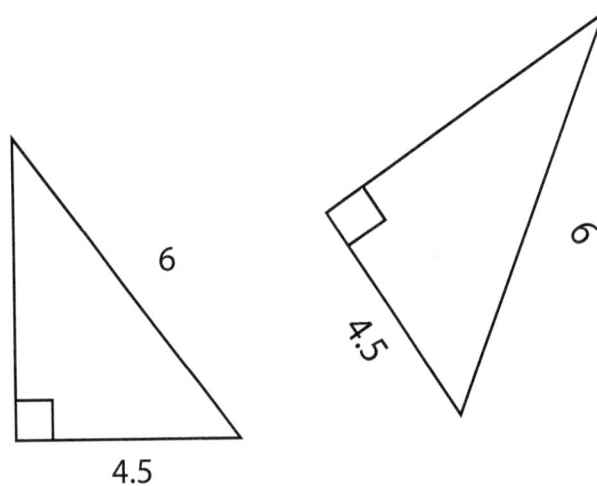

Figure 2

Yes, they are congruent. HL

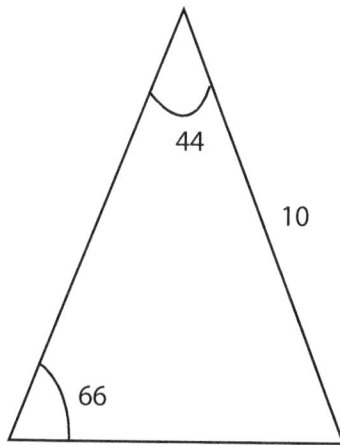

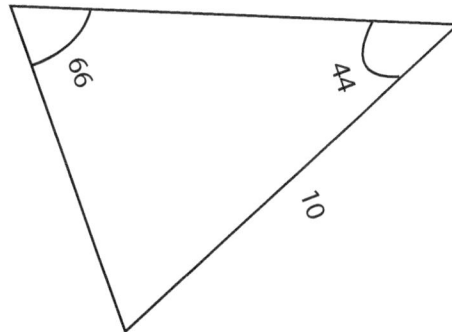

Figure 3

Yes, these are congruent. AAS

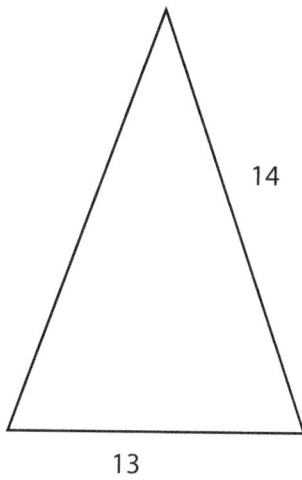

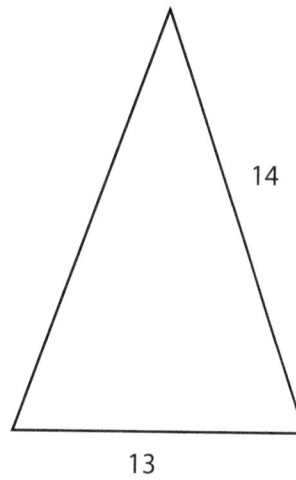

Figure 4

We cannot prove these two triangles are congruent.

Vector Basics; Finding the Magnitude

A vector can be described as a line which has magnitude (The magnitude is essentially the length) and direction. This could be a vector:

You can add vectors simply by connecting them head to tail, and it is important to note that order does not matter in this case. To subtract vectors, simply reverse the direction and add as you normally. To do vectors with an arrow over the letters: $\overrightarrow{AB}$. You may also see them written in bold.

To find the magnitude of vector **a**, denoted $|a|$. The formula is: $|a| = \sqrt{x^2 + y^2 + z^2}$. Let's practice finding the magnitude:

1. <1,2> $\sqrt{5} \approx 2.236$

2. <3,5> $\sqrt{34} \approx 5.831$

3. <4,5> $\sqrt{41} \approx 6.403$

4. <7,7> $7\sqrt{2} \approx 9.899$

5. <9,2> $\sqrt{85} \approx 9.2195$

6. <1,2,6> $\sqrt{41} \approx 6.403$

7. <3,3,6> $3\sqrt{6} \approx 7.3485$

8. <4,5,9> $\sqrt{122} \approx 11.045$

9. <6,7,3> $\sqrt{94} \approx 9.6954$

10. <5,6,9> $\sqrt{142} \approx 11.916$

Corresponding Parts of Congruent Triangles Congruent (CPCTC)

What does CPCTC stand for? Well it stands for, Corresponding Parts of Congruent Triangles Congruent. Sounds like a jumble of words doesn't it? It actually means that if we know that two triangles are congruent, then all of their respective angles and sides are congruent as well. Simple enough?

Write a relationship about the following which can be proven using CPCTC.

We know that $\triangle QRS \cong \triangle TUS$

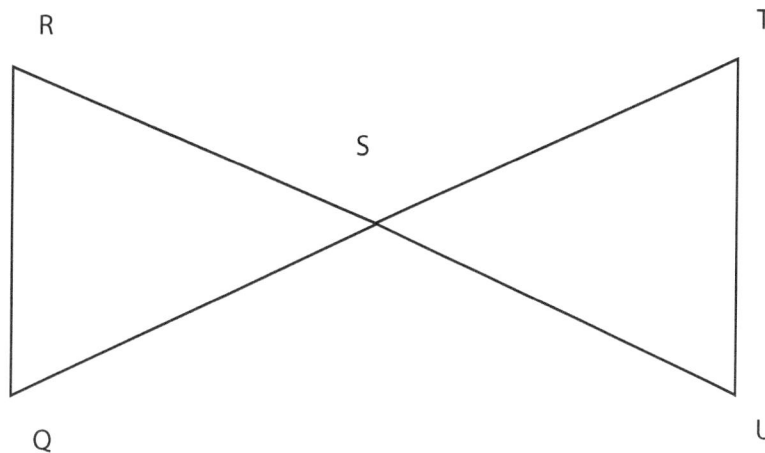

Figure 1

$\overline{RQ} = \overline{TU}$ can be proven using CPCTC.

Use figure 1 for the following:

Write a proof the show that S represents the midpoint of RU and QT, if we know RQ and TU are parallel. Identify which step stands for the CPCTC.

Statements:

$\angle R \cong \angle U$
$US \cong SR$
$\angle RSQ \cong \angle TSU$
$\triangle RSQ \cong \triangle TSU$
$TS \cong SQ$ CPCTC

Sector Area and Arc Length

Trigonometry seems hard enough, but then we have to learn the trigonometry of circles.

Beginning with arc length, we know that an arc is simply a section of the circumference of a circle. Please draw an arc:

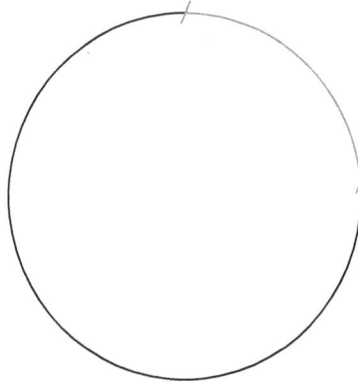

Now, that we can identify an arc, how do we find the length of it? The formula to find the arc length in radians is: $Arc\ Length = \theta r$. To find the arc length in degrees the formula is: $Arc\ Length = \theta r \left(\dfrac{\pi}{180} \right)$.

Use figure 1 to find the arc length (in degrees) of the following:

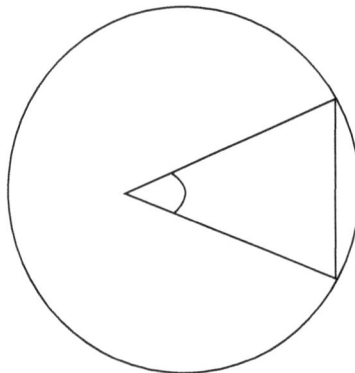

Figure 1

- Find the arc length where $r = 5$ and $\theta = 50$.
- Arc length = 4.363

- Find the arc length where $r = 7$ and $\theta = 66$.
- Arc length = 8.063

- Find the arc length where $r = 10$ and $\theta = 76$.
- Arc length = 8.063

- Find the arc length where $r = 7$ and $\theta = 66$.
- Arc length = 8.063

- Find the arc length where $r = 12$ and $\theta = 88$.
- Arc length = 18.431

- Find the arc length where $r = 7$ and $\theta = 40$.
- Arc length = 4.887

The sector of a circle can be thought of like a piece of the pie. Try drawing and shading in a sector of a circle:

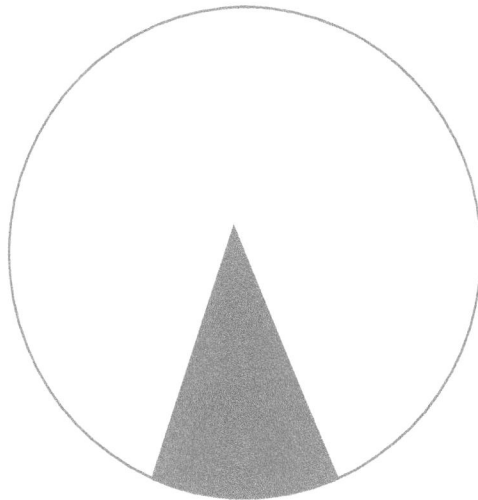

To find the sector of the circle in radians, use the formula: $Sector\ Area = \dfrac{\theta}{2}r^2$. To find the area in degrees: $Sector\ Area = \dfrac{\theta}{360}\pi r^2$.

Use figure 1 to find the sector area (in degrees) for the following:

- Find the arc length where $r = 5$ and $\theta = 50$.

- Sector Area = 10.9

- Find the arc length where $r = 7$ and $\theta = 66$.

- Sector Area = 28.2

- Find the arc length where $r = 10$ and $\theta = 76$. $r = 10\,and\,\theta = 76$.

- Sector Area = 66.3

- Find the arc length where $r = 7$ and $\theta = 66$.

- Sector Area = 28.2

- Find the arc length where $r = 12$ and $\theta = 88$.

- Sector Area=111

- Find the arc length where $r = 7$ and $\theta = 40$.

- Sector Area = 17.1

Arcs and Chords; Finding Chord Length

A chord is a line segment which contains only part of the circle. The diameter is a chord which is through the dead center of the circle. How do we calculate the length of a chord? We calculate the length depending on what we are provided.

- If you are given the central angle and the radius:

$$chord\,length = 2rsin\left(\frac{c}{2}\right)$$

- If you are given the distance to the center and the radius:

$$chord\,length = 2\sqrt{r^2 - d^2}$$

1. $c = 60°$ and $r = 6$

   Chord length = 6

2. $r = 5$ and $d = 6$

   Chord length = 9.798

3. $r = 3$ and $d = 4$

   Chord length = 5.6569

4. $c = 40°$ and $r = 5$

   Chord length = 3.4202

5. $r = 3$ and $d = 5$

   Chord length = 4.4721

6. $r = 5$ and $r = 7$

   Chord length = 9.1652

7. $r = 8$ and $d = 7$

Chord length = 15.875

8. $c = 66°$ and $r = 5$

Chord length = 5.4464

9. $c = 75°$ and $r = 4$

Chord length = 4.8701

10. $c = 54°$ and $r = 5$

Chord length = 4.5399

Composite Figures

Composite figures are those shapes which appear to be made of two or more shapes. Try drawing a composite figure... you could draw a house, an arrow, a space ship. You could draw just about anything.

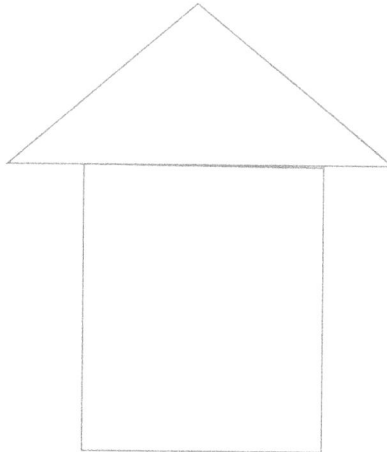

For the following divide the composite shape into its two parts:

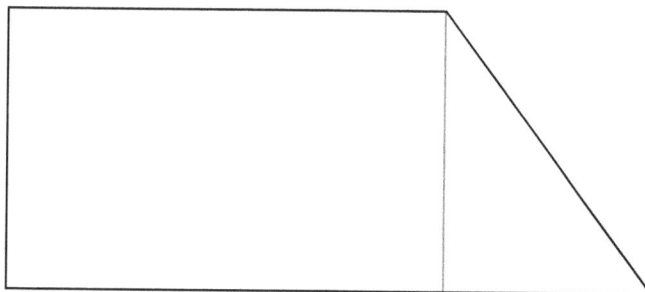

Figure 1

How do we find the area of a composite figure? Simply divide the shape into its respective shapes, calculate the area of each, then sum those individual areas together.

Find the area of the following composite figures:

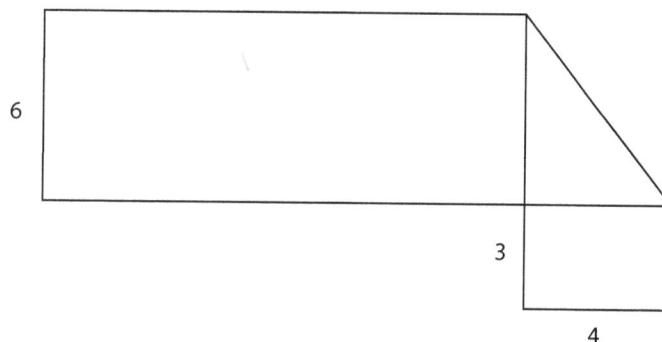

Area=84

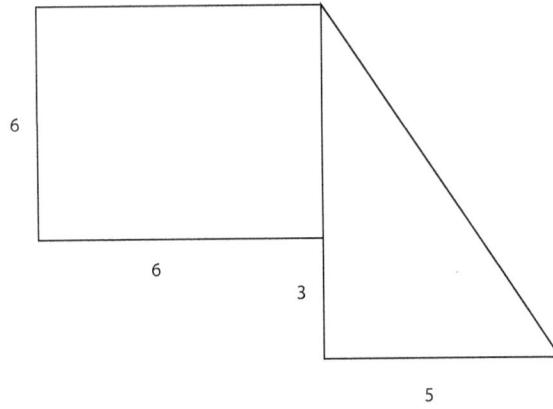

Area=58.5

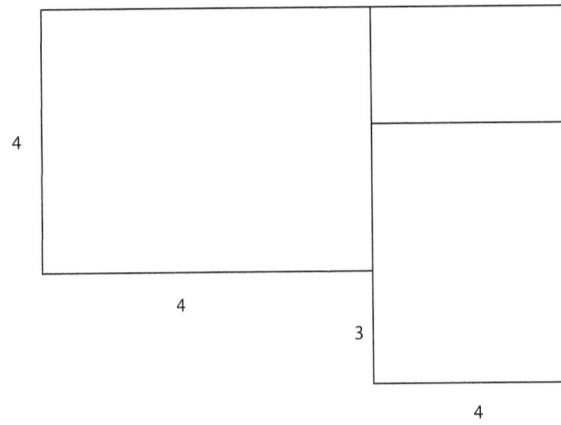

Area=44

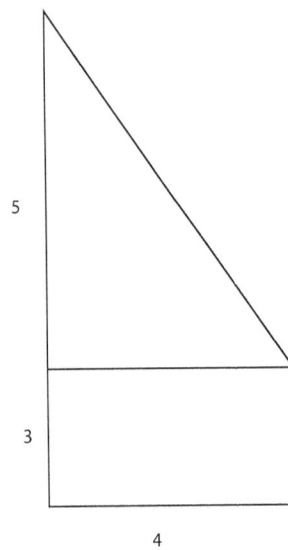

Area=22

The Axiomatic Systems of Geometry

What is an Axiom, or an axiomatic statement? An axiomatic statement is one which is just evidently true. We may also refer to an axiom as a postulate. A theorem is perhaps the most important part of an axiomatic system as it contains the respective proofs. Proofs are the way in which we are able to logically deduce an argument, or a set of premises.

In these systems there are, in fact, some terms which are defined and some which are not. Euclid himself made the attempt to define each and every term, however, we now accept that this is an impossible task.

Please give an example of an undefined term:

Points on a line.

What do you think a perfect axiomatic system might contain?

"A perfect axiomatic system is one which contains all true statements which are derived from a finite axioms."

In **Euclidean geometry** what sort of method is used to prove various theorems?

Constructive proofs

What does it mean to use a constructive proof?

We do not just prove the existence of something, but rather the means by which is was created.

Discuss and Define *Point, Line and Plane.*

"A point is without dimension. It simply represents a specified position, nothing more. A line is one dimension. Lines are defined with a straight line, indicated by a line with corresponding arrows. A plan is two dimensional. Planes are without boundaries, as they are infinite."

Parallel Lines will go on infinitely without ever touching or intersecting.

Perpendicular Lines intersect so that a 90 degree angle is formed at the point of intersection.

Just remember, in order to solve ANY problem in trigonometry, you must only understand these four concepts:

1. Be able to understand the components of a right triangle.

2. Use the given angles to find the respective lengths of sides.

3. The hypotenuse represents the total displacement of distance.

4. Understand how to write and solve for equations with a single variable.

The Distance Formula

Recall that there is an axiom which states that between any two points, there is a line. What if we want to calculate the distance between these two points? We can use the distance formula to calculate the length of the line segment.

The distance formula, given two points (x_1, x_2), (y_1, y_2):

$$Distance = \sqrt{(x_2 - x_1)^2 + (y_2 - y_1)^2}.$$

1. (2, 7), (8, 9)

$D = 6.3246$

2. (4, 7), (6, 3)

$D = 4.4721$

3. (1, 8), (5, 3)

$D = 6.4031$

4. (3, 5), (7, 1)

$D = 5.6569$

5. (5, 5), (4, 4)

$D = 1.4142$

6. (3, 4), (4, 5)

$D = 1.4142$

7. (8, 6), (11, 3)

$D = 4.2426$

8. $(3, 7), (15, 7)$

$D = 12$

9. $(12, 5), (4, 15)$

$D = 12.8062$

10. $(17, 9), (6, 11)$

$D = 11.1803$

The Midpoint Formula

Recall that there is an axiom which states that between any two points, there is a line. What if we want to calculate the distance halfway between these two points? We can use the midpoint formula to calculate the distance exactly half the length of the line segment.

The midpoint formula, given two points (x_1, x_2), (y_1, y_2):

$$Midpoint = \left(\left(\frac{x_1 + x_2}{2} \right), \left(\frac{y_1 + y_2}{2} \right) \right).$$

1. $(2, 7)$, $(8, 9)$

   $(5, 8)$

2. $(4, 7)$, $(6, 3)$

   $(5, 5)$

3. $(1, 8)$, $(5, 3)$

   $(3, 5.5)$

4. $(3, 5)$, $(7, 1)$

   $(5, 3)$

5. $(5, 5)$, $(4, 4)$

   $(4.5, 4.5)$

6. $(3, 4)$, $(4, 5)$

   $(3.5, 4.5)$

7. $(8, 6)$, $(11, 3)$

   $(9.5, 4.5)$

8. (3, 7), (15, 7)

(9, 7)

9. (12, 5), (4, 15)

(8, 10)

10. (17, 9), (6, 11)

(11.5, 10)

Cartesian Coordinate Plane; Practicing Plots

(0,5), (1,6), (2,7), (3,8), (4,8), (5,8), (6,8), (7,8), (7,5), (7,3), (6,1), (5,0), (4,–1), (3,–2), (2,–3), (1,–4), (0,–5), (–1,–4), (–2,–3), (–3,–2), (–4,–1), (–5,0), (–6,1), (–7,3), (–7,5), (–7,8) (–6,8), (–5,8), (–4,8), (–3,8), (–2,7), (–1,6)

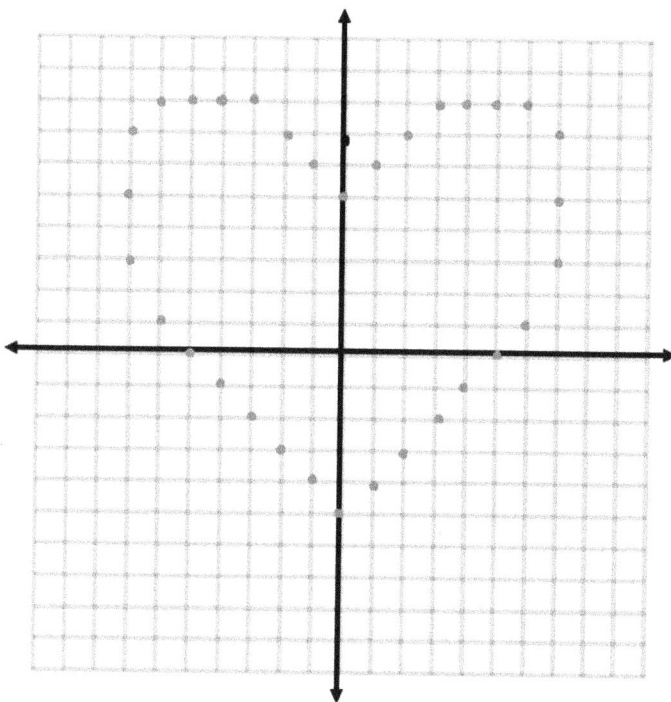

Inverse Trigonometric Ratios

By now we know how to find sin(x), cos(x) or tan(x) How do we find something of the form $a = \sin(x)$? The answer is much simpler than you would think! We simply use inverse trigonometric ratios, in the form $\sin^{-1}(a)$.

We call these the following:

$\sin^{-1}$	$arcsine$
$\cos^{-1}$	$arccosine$
$\tan^{-1}$	$arctangent$

1. $\sin(x) = .482$ *28.12 deg*

2. $\sin(x) = .551$ *33.44 deg*

3. $\cos(x) = .774$ *50.72 deg*

4. $\tan(x) = .88$ *61.64 deg*

5. $\tan(x) = .562$ *34.19 deg*

6. $\cos(x) = .542$ *32.82 deg*

7. $\sin(x) = .321$ *18.72 deg*

8. $\sin(x) = .213$ *12.298 deg*

9. $\cos(x) = .564$ *34.33 deg*

10. $\tan(x) = .977$ *77.69 deg*